Views & Haikus

By

Nino Azcuy

To the never ending

To the iron will

To redeeming my past

To the Uphill

We are new

It was a novel idea

A positive enticement.

But he was trapped in his throat

& Lost in his vices

His efforts were worthless

The black ocean without surface.

Her life gave my heart a rise

Our love, a roller coaster ride.

But sadly,

Our laughter turned into cries

Our butterflies into lies.

We learned to hate, to despise

We were lightning in the skies.

Despite all our tries;

I watched my angel cry,

Black crystals from her eyes.

I guess I'll be going

You didn't care to know me

Solely phones me when lonely

Maybe you'll see one day,

You lost your one and only.

Your words ripped me

But I don't care for sympathy

Nor pity

I'm just angry now

Enough to burn cities.

You bullied me in school

You bullied me online

You did it to be cool

Or when you had the time

I know I was weird.

But I was a nice guy

I just wanted to fit in

To be myself and try

Actual tears I never cried

I never seemed to find the time

I couldn't swallow the pride inside

Instead I just denied

& began telling lies

Or run away and hide in some girl thighs.

Just a kid with a blank stare

Why were you such fiends to me?

You broke my spine.

You buried and defeated me.

All you did was use

& verbally abuse

What you heard is true

My career went boom

I'm writing rhymes and haikus

Refined and fine tuned

But I am still broken

When I'm without you.

All those years

I was made to cry tears

Why was I so weird?

They called me a queer, my bullies revered.

Who was it I feared?

The one in the mirror?

They would chat

About how I was fat

Throw my back pack

Then spat, in my face.

I was rumored bisexual

Now they're more flexible

Say they're pro homosexual.

They kicked me in the testicles

Then said they were Christian?

Seems sort of questionable

When they needed help though, they ran to me.

Who do I speak of?

"My good friends and family."

She went to jail

I almost died

Her face went pale.

suicide.

She tried not to cry

To be the perfect bride

I'd just run away and hide

Deny my lies until the pain would subside.

I was so impressed

She took away my breath

My wicked princess;

The witch in a dress.

Are you...

this hurt I have kept?

This thorn in my stem?

Because ever since you left,

I have pains in my chest.

I now have good sense

To old friends who were traitorous

Be careful

When my mind is clear;

That's when I'm most dangerous.

When life is at its hardest

Look to where your heart is

You'll find God there,

& you'll have strength in darkness.

I pray these words are meaningful

Then maybe his ego could

Use letters as the needles

To atone for his evils.

Sleeping next to her

I'm finally at peace

It feels as if,

I can finally breathe

My soul is at ease.

Her dark skin

Her eyes like crystals

Even after a day

I always miss those.

I don't know why

With her I even try

So many times; I tried to say goodbye

She doesn't let me kiss her

But I am not breathing

Unless I am with her

You are so above me

How could you love me?

What is it with you?

Why can't you trust me?

Even love is short handed

Why are the ones most precious?

Always taken for granted.

I hang only by a thread

Every day feels so long

I'm too in my head

With you I broke through

May my thanks be to you.

I hold you most dear

& if your near;

With me in here...

So long to my fears.

A young man waiting to get old

"God is there for you"

I'm told.

But there I was ready to fold.

I guess I should thank you.

For keeping me warm in the cold.

You are a giant.

I am a bumblebee

You could have smothered me,

But chose to love me.

I can never repay

All that you've done for me.

Don't be afraid

To live, to relate

To love, and to hate.

To be happy, to feel pain.

To feel insane

To feel shame

You're only human, we're all the same

Just pray

It's okay.

The darkest cloud began to surround

A spiritual shroud that just came down

It covered around, the people in town.

Taking a toll as it swallowed the souls.

Who made this new specimen?

The doctors with medicines.

His opinions were weak

His arrogance peaked

Blinded by perceptions

He could barely see.

The serpents wrapped his neck,

like a blue berry tree.

On his hands and knees, he shouts at the seas.

God set him free

A breath of relief.

Anger, regrets,

all your inner demons.

Refuse to see them.

Focus on happiness.

It's everlasting freedoms.

When you're happy.

Your heart is smiling

So just enjoy it.

The sun is shining.

Today.

When you're staring

I'm watching you blink

I love your dark eyes,

And nails painted pink.

Can you ever love me one day?

What do you think?

Sometimes you're scary

Sometimes you're so sweet

I'm watching you breathe

An Angel Asleep

God help me up.

Give me the luck

Make me a King.

An Author Above.

Truth or dare was an art

Nervous Sex in the dark

The movies then the park.

 we were so far from smart.

May your looks never depart.

I held your hands at thirteen

But you still hold my heart.

You said you sealed your fate

Old man, you did it.

I hope you enjoyed all your break

But you aren't done yet

A final marker to make.

Trust me

Anger just makes you ugly.

Trust me

Rage makes one disgusting.

I would beg

I would plead

On my legs, on my knees.

On the twelfth of December;

God's hands set me free.

Don't worry at night

Just do what's right

& at the end of your life;

You will see the light.

I know what it's like

To get picked on in life

Made to feel like

You can do nothing right.

To be stabbed with a knife;

In the darkest of night.

You see no end in sight

You can lay down and die....

Or you can get up and fight!

I know I mess up

But you know I care for you.

Don't be so heartless

You know that I'm scared of you.

Different temperatures,

for different needs

Different tasks,

for different breeds.

Different paths, for different beings.

But forget all of that.

Just remember to do good acts.

To do good deeds.

You're far to flexible.

Your morals deemed sellable

Your smaller than a decimal of a fragmented decibel.

But anyone can change.

You can still be incredible.

No woman to call my own

My queen left her throne a long time ago.

Just an empty home all alone

Please

Please pick up the phone.

Blessed are those;

Who take personal responsibility.

They blame God and each other.

The hypocrisy's killing me.

Choked by my addictions;

Cursed with infernal inflictions.

Perhaps by changing my decisions

May I be freed from these prisons.

An image is worthless

But for wisdom keep searching

You're perfectly okay

Not being perfect.

Don't do it alone

Don't let failure repeat

It's okay to use crutches,

as you regain your feet.

A poem doesn't need to rhyme

Or be a dozen lines

It doesn't have to be divine,

Or fit a design.

It needs to be read by the right mind

At the right time.

I know you'll do well

I think they'll like it just fine

Write.

Her poster of Paris

She watched her dreams parish

She was never embarrassed

She was reckless and careless.

Why didn't our paths cross?

I could have seen us in marriage.

I spent all that time

Searching for something.

We all had absolutely nothing.

That time was a blessing

A constant youthful questioning

The beautiful quest;

for everything.

I gave her my coat

A cold throat at the end of her rope.

Her beauty fading in cigarette smoke.

She's still dreaming

Of Paris and hope.

Her dreams may be dying;

But the room keeps her afloat.

My illness, my fight

My darkness, your light

My war

The fight

On January 9th

God saved my life.

Amidst a life crisis

He's trying to regroup

He wants to recoup,

But doesn't know what to do.

He can't swallow the truth.

He's bathing in pain

He's drowning in truth

We must keep humility

I was so used to winning

I wouldn't swallow defeat.

It's okay to retreat

To know when you're beat.

Although I was a liar,

You didn't depart

Real friends from the start

It's hard to see in front

When you live in the dark.

I just need the fire

That I had in the start.

How can we have strength?

With the pain in our hearts.

My whole life was taken

The earth beneath me had shaken

At the beginning I was mistaken.

I thought in struggle I was strong

I was in denial all along.

The more I tried to gain

The more that it was gone.

Slutty women and my vanity

Nightly drug use and calamity.

Bigger lies

My humanity.

Betrayal from my family.

Life

is dark insanity

Hope is a concept for the weak

Those in denial of defeat.

To help them sleep under the sheets.

Life is like blood in the streets

A constant flowing of defeat.

There is a God though

Somewhere up there

He loves me too.

I am beautiful

In my own wicked ways.

Why did you wake me up?

Was it to say sorry?

Was it to say I love you?

Or both?

It's good for me.

But bad for her.

I just feel bad, for the insecure.

She's so unsure.

If anyone's noticed her

But my eyes haven't left.

I'm still catching my breath

If only for now

This is my body

I have existed

What a gift to be lifted.

I don't deserve God help

I beg for another second.

But as my vitals collapse

I just might get it.

I cannot see you.

But you are so beautiful

Not for what they say

Not for what they think

Not for all the stories.

Just because you are

To me.

A long time it took him

Just a kid with big dreams

So big

He didn't know where to put them.

Make sure for certain

That these words serve their purpose.

I love you so much

You erased all the hurting

Through this.

The sun came out

Again.

I can feel the fire coming to an end. I don't know what the point of all this was but I'm trying to bend. I believe in God; but I don't know what these words mean for my purpose. I still have the days, the days when I am worthless. I made this book thinking my life would change. Thinking I would earn some respect. But the day never came; failure feels like a trend. Maybe it's the end, of a failed prototype. Maybe it's the journey, or the one of its kind. I will go with the wind. I understand that I'm small. I won't live with "what ifs". I'll take pride in them all.

My Poetry.

www.ingramcontent.com/pod-product-compliance
Lightning Source LLC
Chambersburg PA
CBHW060719030426
42337CB00017B/2926